THE WOMAN
IN THE NEXT BOOTH

poems by
Jo McDougall

 BkMk PRESS-UMKC
College of Arts & Sciences
University of Missouri-Kansas City

Acknowledgements

"At the Vietnam War Memorial for the American Dead" first appeared in *Southern Poetry Review.* "A Farm Wife Laments Her Husband's Absence" and "Act" first appeared in *Nimrod.* "When the Buck or Two Steakhouse Changed Hands" appeared in *Chimerical.* "The Black and Small Birds of Remorse" appeared in *New Mexico Humanities Review* and *Patterns of Poetry: an Encyclopedia of Forms,* Miller Williams, editor (LSU Press). "Coming Back, I Visit Myself" appeared in *Poetry Miscellany.* An earlier version of "1942" appeared in *Review.* "The Bluebird Cafe" and "Something, Anything" appeared in *Jumping Pond: Poems & Stories from the Ozarks,* Burns & Sanders, eds. "The 875" appeared in *The Maine Times.* "Walking Down Prospect" appeared in *Intro 13.* "The Menial" appeared in *The Arkansas Times.* "A Lady Charged with Involuntary Manslaughter" appeared in *White River Literary Arena.* "The Day After the Bottomlands Farmer Lost His Wife," "Things That Will Keep," "Labor Day," and earlier versions of "Hearing Tractors" (formerly entitled "A New Life") and "The Privileged" appeared in *Louisiana Literature.* "The House Facing Dahlia" appeared in *The Texas Review.*

Many of these poems also appeared in the chapbook *Women Who Marry Houses,* Coyote Love Press, Portland, Maine, 1983.

Typography by Michael Annis.
Cover & jacket illustration by Herb Bryant.
Jacket & book design by Pat Huyett.

Library of Congress Cataloging-in-Publication Data
McDougall, Jo.
  The woman in the next booth.

  I. Title
PS3563.C3586W6   1987   811'.54   87-70661
ISBN 0-933532-64-4

For my mother's memory and for my father,
with special thanks
to Miller and to Jim

CONTENTS

THE WOMAN
IN THE NEXT BOOTH

Walking Down Prospect

I walk down Prospect
behind the building with the Gothic windows.
Inside me your names fly up like two quail.
When they are gone
I pull my coat around me.
When I get home
I try to call you.
Where you are in the world now it is dark.
The phone rings into that.

Labor Day

The boy's mother hears it on the radio.
A fishing boat has been found.
She walks through the house,
reassuring the backs of chairs.

Her husband comes from the lake.
Dusk filters through the screen.
Sit down, he says.
He puts his hat on the table.

The Black and Small Birds of Remorse

come in the cool hours
one by one
to perch on the backs of chairs.
Anywhere you are trying to start over —
tossing green salad, changing white sheets —
they glide in of a sudden,
shift from foot to foot.

Silly Women

When death sees a silly woman
he ambles over
and asks her to dance.
If she says Thank you no
he puts his hand on her shoulder anyway
turns her around
teaches her an old step
or two.

Death likes silly women
who believe the names he gives them
who will be ready when he wants to go
who dance a little closer than they should.

Settlement

They had a house.
They had her mother's mantel clock
and his grandfather's bed.
When he left he took nothing belonging to him.
He has been gone a long time.
Today a letter comes.
He will sell her the rocker she gave him one Christmas,
and the bed.
She responds.
She will sell him the mantel clock.
She is careful to say
she has had the clock repaired.
It keeps better time.

Women Who Marry Houses

have lost husbands
to time or to other women.
They look for smaller houses
with hipped roofs.
They move into neighborhoods with large trees.
Women who marry houses
are fond of the dark
when the house cracks its knuckles.

Act

Towards the last my aunt writes
all the hymns she knows
on little slips of paper
and tapes them onto the lampshade
beside her bed.
She says she does this to test her mind.
It makes the light dim.

The 875

In Gillett, a town in Arkansas,
on January twelfth of every year
eight hundred and seventy-five citizens
buy tickets for platters of raccoon and rice.

Trappers bring in the coons, skinned,
the legs gone except for one
ending in the little hand
to make certain that no dog
or cat has been run in.

A Lady Charged with Involuntary Manslaughter Says

it will go bad
but you won't know when.
Say some night,
driving fast along the flats of Kansas,
not too fast,
thinking back,
     You were
     Brushing your hair,
     Taking off your clothes,
     Pouring a Scotch

The car takes a hill, reaches the top.
Something there, maybe not,
the shadow of a cloud, cast by the moonlight,
or something in your headlights, kneeling.

Men

She waits in the car and watches two men
try to sell a truck
to the man who brought her here.
He slams the truck's good door
and lifts the hood.
The men talk,
looking at the ground
as though they were reading something.
She leans back in the car,
glad to be in the company of men.

The Bessemer

We called the building
my father housed the Bessemer in
the pumping shed.
Loretta and Horace
lived in the lean-to beside the shed
so that Horace could listen for
a shift in the Bessemer's sound.
He had to keep it running, day and night,
to water my father's rice fields.

Because of the noise it made in the lean-to,
nobody could talk.
When Loretta set the table for supper,
vibration from the engine
wrinkled the milk.

One morning Loretta went into a part of the shed
where Horace had told her not to go.
Her sleeve was caught
in the belt of the Bessemer.   Or so
we suppose.   Horace found her.
Over the noise
nobody heard her when she screamed.

Harlot Hag Dry Harpie

A woman from Opelousas
came to live
with a barker from Royal American Shows
who had lived with an alligator lady, and Siamese twins.
So the woman from Opelousas
would sometimes paint a harelip on herself,
tape down an eyelid, paint her nose black, sleep on all fours.
Once she tied her ankle to her thigh
and hopped over to him and did his will.

On those nights he could go on forever.
On those nights he'd chant a crawling song,
Pomegranate sequin dove my harlot hag dry harpie,
as he would cradle her head against his face
he'd painted purple
for her
and he would cry.
She'd lick his tears, he'd rock her:
Jesus Mother Mary Martha Tessie Christ Lord Love

The Professor of Chinese Dialects
In a Small University Town in Ohio

hears the 5:15 from Akron
slide toward the single strip
of the tiny airport.
Standing at the kitchen table
he makes himself one drink,
unfolds and folds his paper.
After supper his wife goes into the bedroom
goes naked to bed
goes slowly to sleep.

The man sits in the next room, translating Li Po.
He does not see the moon that Li Po speaks of
or the woman.
Under the eaves the night birds
rustle like taffeta.

Something, Anything

The way Mrs. Jensen slams the window shut
in the apartment above says
I'm alive.
Also
Krebbs at the bench on Maple and 3rd
shows off his new teeth.
Irma Bailey is swiping a dirty menu
from the Cafe Royale
to show to Mrs. Payton who's never been there.

Pilgrims, we may not make it.

Reporting Back

There has been an accident.
A bridge has collapsed.   The water under it
has taken a bus, a car, a truck.
For days we watch a picture
of the one survivor
who fell with his truck tucked around him, two hundred feet,
to bounce off a passing freighter.
The man will not talk with reporters
or answer his phone.

Some who see what they see will never tell
say they don't remember
say what somebody said they said.
Buy this man a drink.
Ask him
what did you think of going down?
Hydrangeas?   Your mother?   A fox?
"A fox," he says.

One Mile Out of New Smyrna

you begin to see signs.
A dog crosses the road.
A turtle touches the pavement
and turns back.
A truck with a loose tarp passes;
the tarp reaches out.

The next morning you wake up afraid.

At the Vietnam War Memorial

For the American Dead

she finds her son's name.
He comes towards her and grins.
She sees him
step out onto the driveway by the house,
dribble a basketball,
make three perfect hook shots
into the goal his father helped him hang.
She had forgotten how big his hands were.

Silence rocks through her like a train.

The Bluebird Cafe

Eating alone
I shuffle a magazine
turn the coffee cup
light a cigarette.
There is no one here except for one
waitress, a cook I can't see,
me, and one old woman in a booth.
Why didn't you come home last night?

Before the Doctor Says
What He Has to Say

My sister and I go into the room
where our mother is dying.
She will not turn her face from the window.
She gestures as if there is someone she knows
on the hospital lawn.
We realize
we no longer come first in her life.

Before the doctor says what he has to say
we believe she is merely distant,
that we can reach to pull her back
the way as children we waded to our small boat
anchored in the shallows,
rocking and waiting for us.

In The Visitors' Room

In the visitors' room
of a Georgia institution
a woman talks to a man
who pretends to sleep or pretends to listen.

Upstairs
someone is running a vacuum cleaner
back and forth.

The Voice of the Radio Announcer

invites us to tea
wears white gloves
opens an ivory envelope:
    A Camden man was drowned early this morning
    The dismembered body of a Huntsville woman
    was found in the rental lockers
    at a downtown station

The voice gets into a black car
signals to the driver
slides the glass closed.

Works

A sharecropper's wife
says her gratitude politely
to the Methodist woman
who brings canned goods and bread
in a Safeway sack.
When the woman leaves,
the wife slams the door, startling
two pictures on the wall.

The Menial

Each woman keeps another woman —
Old, painted, with spittle on her chin —
Who comes through a small gate when we call her
To cook, to clean our teeth
To suckle our young
Even to bed down in our names
To make love in our names
To have our children
She will do almost anything except
Dig in the ground a rectangle
Sink into that a box with a lid
Climb into that naked.

Things That Will Keep

On my father's desk sits a 1920's vase
in the shape of Loie Fuller, dancing,
and a picture of my mother
smiling from some town nobody remembers.
My father likes to tell
how she bought the vase with egg money
in the Great Depression
and a set of books for me.
They had blue spines.

Today, the morning of her funeral,
it is winter and my mother wears a sensible dress.
Women come into her kitchen
bearing casseroles, molded salads,
things that will keep.
Behind each visitor
my father shuts and shuts the door.

O summer of backyards and sparrows
RedRoverComeOver
O dark after cicadas
that brought my mother watchful to the screen.

Winter Room

The room you wake up in is a winter room.
The man you love has come in a dream
to wave goodbye from a 1950 Buick.
You push the cat off the bed
and slide your feet to the floor.
With a cup of coffee on the end of the ironing board
you spread a blouse,
making it ready for the reassuring steam.
Every day you will do something for the last time.

To a Man in Kansas

I'm doing the dishes in Winooski, Vermont
and thinking of you.
These are not your children in the next room.
These are not your dishes.
From Wichita my sister writes
to say she planted larkspur on your grave.
I watch a crow standing still beside the road.
Before I finish the dishes the crow is gone.
It is going to rain tomorrow.
I marry you again.

Coming Back, I Visit Myself

I knock twice on the door
of the old apartment.
A woman lets me in.
My silver toiletries.   My plants.
My knife and fork and napkin.
I look to see what has died or been given away
but everything is here.

I say nothing.
I am not supposed to say anything.
I poke my head in the closet
looking for the good green dress.

Watching

I watch a hawk turn,
dropping the sun off its wings.

My mother stared at the darkness
that sat on her hands.
At the end
she tried to shake it loose.

Next Door

Next door the old man and the old woman come out
as they do every day
for a walk to the corner and back.
They pause at the edge of the porch.
Down one step, he turns to the woman
and waits.
I think she is trying to remember
where they are going.

I wish I were first
in your life again.

For T.

You have been dead four days
and nothing comforts me except
that crow on the lawn, foraging.

The Paper Xylophone

You witness your madness.
First you build the xylophone from paper
in your office.
Then the feathered nose-piece.
You send for a parakeet.
You begin not to answer your phone.
After knocking, friends go away.
Needing the right sound,
you snap the parakeet
like a bean.

The Tractor Driver's Funeral

I go because he worked on my father's farm.
The pall bearers' coats are too loose or too tight.
What the widow wears is
pink and wrong.
At the cemetery I touch her
but she doesn't remember.

I lie on my bed and drop my shoes to the floor.
In the bathroom my husband brushes his teeth.
I put on the black gown.

A Woman Married to Grief

When they met, the woman didn't think
it would last.
She said to herself she would tire of him after awhile.

She knows now that she will never leave.
She has become proud to be seen with him.
Whenever they go out,
she puts on a hat with a wide brim.

Remembering a Sunny Climate

The old woman folds clothes
and puts them away
while the old man naps on the couch.
They have said nothing to each other all day,
but in the woman's mind they talk as they did
and work in the vineyards
and stir in each other's arms at night
while the pear trees drop their blooms.

Emerson County Shaping Dream

Any girl in Emerson County
knows what dreams are for —
Daddy in the shape of a rich boy.
She chooses him who chooses her,
dreamed in the shape of his mama.
Their house is happy
if the girl is pretty, if he likes the things
she says to him,
if the boy has land from his daddy, flat, not hilly,
if she loves the way he loves on her.
The bank holds all their papers
but nobody mentions this.
One day
a man from a neighboring county
smiles at the girl.
They begin to meet
at the Albert Pick, or the Claridge.
Nobody mentions this either.

Audiences

Audiences are so lonely
as the curtain falls
on the groom and bride or
the opera star or the corpse.
The lights go up and those in the audience
raise their eyes.
They talk softer or louder,
knowing they address a dark
into which those important ones are gone.
They head for home, for coffee, for a phone.
It doesn't matter.

Becoming Invisible

a found poem, from the archives of Arkansas folklore

It is possible to become invisible.
Follow a few simple steps.
First, you catch a toad.
Put it in a clay planter,
the type with a hole in the bottom.
The first full moon
take it out to the graveyard.
Find a grave with an ant hill on it.
Put the toad on the ant hill;
cover it with the pot.
The next full moon
go back and get the toad's bones.
Take them home and stand in front of a mirror.
Place the bones
one at a time in your mouth
until you find the one that makes you invisible.

There are 192 bones in a toad.

The House Facing Dahlia

In the house next door facing Dahlia,
Ardeliah Soames—whose front yard flourished
    with sunflower whirligigs,
cement flamingoes, and a cat she called Malone—
died today.

Saturdays there had come a black boy mowing the lawn,
each Saturday for three years or so.
She called the boy Floyd.   His name was Foster.

Today, in a tie and suit
Foster came after they took Mrs. Soames away.
He weeded both sides of the walk.

Foster took a sunflower as he left
and one of the pink flamingoes,
still inclined and delicate
under his arm.

The Day After the Bottomlands Farmer Lost His Wife

he brought a hired woman to the house
to cook his meals.
People talked.   She was not the customary black,
but a white woman off the river
who smoked, who wore, winter and summer,
Red Ball boots.
She and the farmer almost never spoke.
After supper
she cleared the table
and set it for breakfast.
She put cornbread on a plate
beneath a napkin
and turned his water glass
mouth down.

Stopping My Car for the Light

Stopping my car for the light,
I smile as a man and a dog cross the street.
I smile because they don't know who I am
or that you are gone;
also because
the man is apparently not thinking anything
and the dog stops to yawn.

Between the Wars

To be a stranger
is to arrive maybe in Bangor,
stepping into a diner
at noon.
No one else is in the diner
except a man and a woman
dancing with their eyes closed.
The juke box is playing "For All We Know."

After Seeing a Movie
About the American Bombing
of Cambodia

Undressing for bed, I think about Cambodia's grief.
That isn't true;
I think about you, gone,
and no way to find you.

You may be eating now, or reading a paper
in a room I'll never see.
The wisteria we planted
has twisted its way to the roof.

After the Quarrel

My car follows yours
down the mountain road
scattering crows and gravel.
At the highway we turn
our backs to one another.

A Farm Wife Laments
Her Husband's Absence

At sunset the house cools, popping.
The snow that began last night
went on all day.
Snow climbs the windows.
It covers everything:
the hedge behind the house, the barn,
the poplar tree taller than the barn.
When the snow stops
I inch the 4x4 into town
knowing you're not there.
But a man getting out of his car
pushes his hair back
the way you do.

The Other Side

My mother dresses chickens.
My father reads.
I call to them.
They glance up, annoyed.

Hearing Tractors

After the bank takes the farm,
the farmer's wife goes back, invisible,
to live there again.
She watches the owners
take down the kitchen curtains.
She watches them plant peonies along the walk.
In town, her body believes
it waxes the old furniture,
hears tractors
in the traffic far below her window.

When the Buck or Two Steakhouse Changed Hands

They put plastic over the menus.
They told the waitresses to wear white shoes.
They fired Rita.
They threw out the unclaimed keys
and the pelican with a toothpick
that bowed as you left.

1942

My father's harmonica came off the mantel every night.
He played it while my mother sang
until they went to bed.
The last songs were always
Working on the Railroad, O Susanna,
and *Sam,* a song my mother invented.
Whenever the paper said
someone in our town was killed
or missing in action,
my father wouldn't take the harmonica down
even if
it was no one we knew.

A Girl in a Sundress

enters a cafe.
A woman drinking beer in a booth
remembers one August, one Sunday.

A fresh dress
stiff with starch.
All afternoon she waits for him by the lake.
That night lying under the fan
she promises not to let it
happen again.

The girl in the sundress
looks at the woman
but not as if there is anything between them.

Dancing Man

The music in Mick's Bar tonight
is three parts smoke and one part hard down blues.
The man who brought me is drinking bourbon shots and beer.
The woman in the next booth shouts
Play something for me Play something slow for me.

I turn for another drink
and one of the men on the dance floor
has on your brown hat,
three guinea feathers in the hat band.
You are in Mexico, or Greece.

I would leave with him,
let him do whatever he wanted to do
if he would keep the hat on.

The Privileged

They homestead
a square of harsh country
in the Maine of their imagination.

Almost every week
they dig potatoes in sleet.
300 miles from the nearest doctor,
the baby dies in fever;
the horse dies too.

They will never give it up,
that place where he gives her bruises big as pears,
where she scratches
blood-pearls and blooms on his face.

How else can they endure,
two privileged people
in a town just west of Topeka
the wheat fields, the houses with wide porches
lying all about them?

Progress

I stand beside my mother's winter grave.

I consider that when I have slipped into that darkness
and then been followed there by my children and theirs
she will not cross anybody's mind.

I touch the earth exactly, I think, above her heart.

The Gift

Fireflies send their codes from the grass
like signals from a difficult coast.

I want to thank you
for climbing the steep road to my cabin,
for bringing wine,
for humming off-key in the dark.

Here is a book with all the letters of our names.

Jo McDougall, a native of the Arkansas Delta, now lives in Little Rock. She is also the author of the poetry collections *From Darkening Porches* and *Towns Facing Railroads*, three chapbooks, and the monograph *Roots and Recognition: Where Poetry Comes From*. She has taught at Pittsburg State University in Kansas and Northeast Louisiana University. She has held three MacDowell Colony fellowships, and her poetry has appeared in such journals as *The Kenyon Review*, *The Hudson Review*, *New Orleans Review*, and *New Letters*. Her work has most recently been anthologized in *The Made Thing: An Anthology of Contemporary Southern Poetry* and *Arkansas, Arkansas: 1970-Present* (Vol. II). She is now working on a memoir and has just completed her fourth poetry collection. A film based on McDougall's dramatic monologues is scheduled for release in the summer of 2000. She holds an MFA in creative writing (poetry) from the University of Arkansas.